laugh yourself silly
VALENTINES
day joke and riddle book for kids

HAZEL LAWSON

laugh yourself silly
VALENTINES
day joke and riddle book for kids

Celebrate Valentine's Day with a dash of mystery and a sprinkle of giggles! Engage in heartwarming fun with these 100 charming riddles and jokes, perfect for kids aged 7-13.

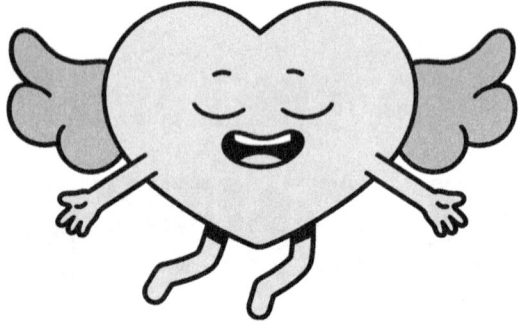

HAZEL LAWSON

COPYRIGHT © 2023 All rights reserved. This book or any portion thereof may not be reproduced or used in any manner whatsoever without the express written permission of the publisher except for the use of brief quotations in a book review. Printed in the United States of America

Welcome to a world of giggles and heartwarming joy!

In this enchanting Valentine's Day joke and riddle book for kids, laughter takes center stage as Cupid's arrows deliver a payload of delightful humor.

Brace yourselves for a delightful journey filled with chuckles, snickers, and contagious grins. Each page is a treasure trove of funny love quips, cute puns, and adorable jokes that will tickle your heart.

Whether you're a little cupid or a budding comedian, this collection promises laughter till your cheeks turn rosy.

Share the joy, spread the smiles, and get ready to Laugh Yourself Silly every hilarious moment in this special edition just for you!

HAZEL LAWSON

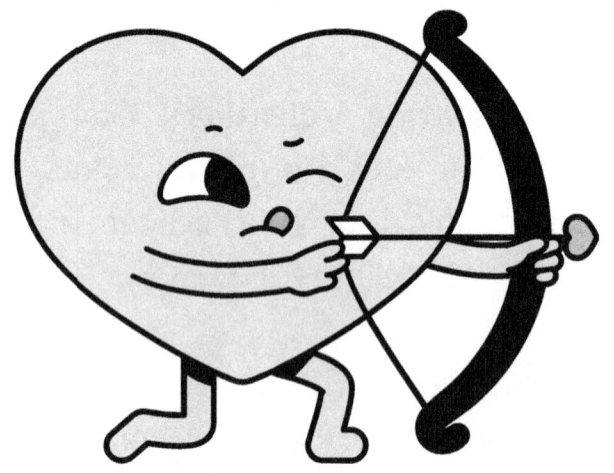

VALENTINES day jokes

In this section of the book you will find some fun Valentines Day jokes.

Get ready for some awesome laughs and giggles. You can answer these alone or with friends.

Q1.

Why did the Valentine's Day card go to school?

ANSWER

Because it wanted to be a smartie!

Q2.

What did one bee say to the other on Valentine's Day?

ANSWER

Bee-Mine!

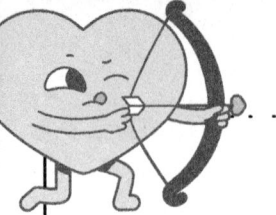

Q3.

Why did the banana go out with the prune on Valentine's Day?

ANSWER

Because it couldn't find a date!

Q4.

What did the stamp say to the envelope on Valentine's Day?

ANSWER

Stick with me, and we'll go places!

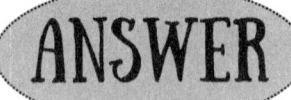

Q5.

Why did the teddy bear say no to dessert?

ANSWER

It was already stuffed!

Q6.

What did one plate say to another plate?

ANSWER

Tonight, dinner is on me!

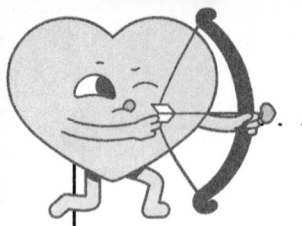

Q7.

What did the boy cat say to the girl cat on Valentine's Day?

ANSWER

"You're purr-fect for me!"

Q8.

Why was the belt arrested on Valentine's Day?

ANSWER

It was holding up a pair of pants!

Q9.

What did the boy cat say to the girl cat on Valentine's Day?

ANSWER

"You're purr-fect for me!"

Q10.

What did one chocolate say to the other on Valentine's Day?

ANSWER

"You're sweet!"

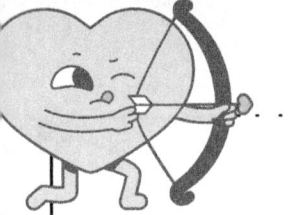

Q11.

What did the French chef give his wife on Valentine's Day?

ANSWER

A hug and a quiche!

Q12.

What do you call a bear with no teeth on Valentine's Day?

ANSWER

A gummy bear!

Q13.

Why did the bicycle fall over on Valentine's Day?

ANSWER

It was two-tired!

Q14.

What's a vampire's favorite fruit on Valentine's Day?

ANSWER

A blood orange!

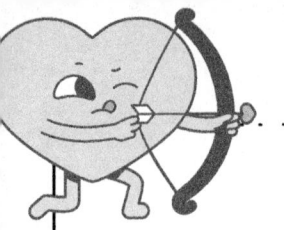

Q15.

What did the boy pencil say to the girl pencil on Valentine's Day?

ANSWER

"You're write for me!"

Q16.

What did one volcano say to the other on Valentine's Day?

ANSWER

I lava you!

Q17.

What did the calculator say to its sweetheart on Valentine's Day?

ANSWER

"You can count on me!"

Q18.

How did the phone propose to his girlfriend on Valentine's Day?

ANSWER

He gave her a ring!

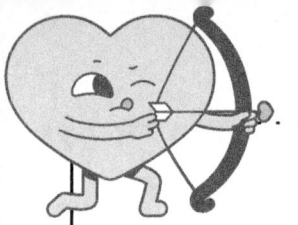

Q19.

What do you call two birds in love?

ANSWER

Tweet-hearts!

Q20.

Why did the banana go out with the prune on Valentine's Day?

ANSWER

Because it couldn't find a date!

Q21.

What do you call a very small valentine?

ANSWER

A valen-tiny!

Q22.

Why did the cookie go to the doctor on Valentine's Day?

ANSWER

It was feeling crumbly!

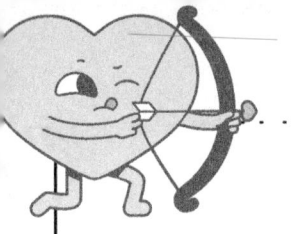

Q23.

What did one pickle say to another on Valentine's Day?

ANSWER

"You mean a great dill to me!"

Q24.

What did the boy owl say to the girl owl on Valentine's Day?

ANSWER

"Owl be yours!"

Q25.

What did one volcano say to the other on Valentine's Day?

ANSWER

"You rock my world!"

Q26.

What do you call two birds in love who stick together?

ANSWER

Vel-crows!

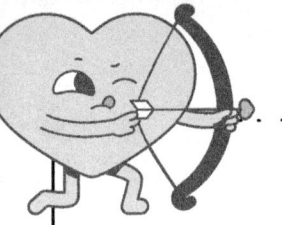

Q27.

Why did the grape stop in the middle of the road on Valentine's Day?

ANSWER

Because it ran out of juice!

Q28.

What did one cupcake say to the other on Valentine's Day?

ANSWER

You're the icing on the cake!

Q29.

Why did the bee have a lot of Valentine's Day admirers?

Because it was the "bee's knees"!

Q30

Why should you date a goalie?

Because they are a "keeper".

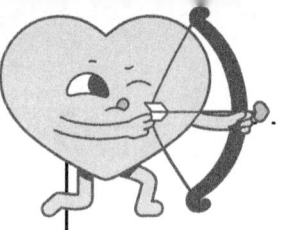

Q31.

Why did the spider go on a date on Valentine's Day?

ANSWER

It wanted to find its perfect web-mate!

Q32.

What did one hat say to the other on Valentine's Day?

ANSWER

"You suit me well!"

Q33.

What did one wall say to the other on Valentine's Day?

ANSWER

"I love hanging out with you!"

Q34.

What did one strawberry say to another on Valentine's Day?

ANSWER

"You're berry special to me!"

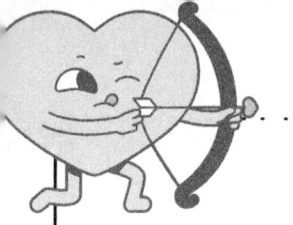

Q35.

What did the grape say to the raisin on Valentine's Day?

ANSWER

"You're getting all wrinkled up!"

Q36.

What did the hat say to the scarf on Valentine's Day?

ANSWER

You warm my heart!

Q37.

What did the boy light bulb say to the girl light bulb on Valentine's Day?

ANSWER

I love you watts and watts!

Q38.

What did the frog say to his Valentine?

ANSWER

"I'm hopping you'll be mine!"

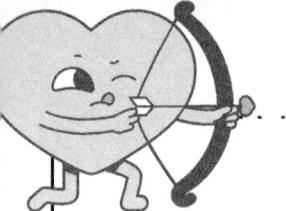

Q39.

What did one ocean say to the other ocean on Valentine's Day?

ANSWER

"Nothing, they just waved!"

Q40.

Why did the bee get married?

ANSWER

Because it found its "honey".

Q41.

Why did the pair of oars fall in love?

ANSWER

Because they are "row" mantic

Q42.

Why do kids put candy under their pillow for Valentines Day?

ANSWER

To have "Sweet" dreams.

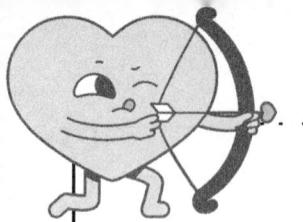

Q43.

What did the bat say to his valentine?

ANSWER

You're fun to hang around

Q44.

What does a boy ghost call its Valentine?

ANSWER

A "ghoul-friend"

Q45.

Why do skunks love valentines day?

ANSWER

Because they are "scent-a-mental".

Q46.

What did the ghost say to its valentine?

ANSWER

You are "boo-tiful"!

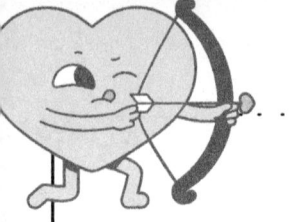

Q47.

How can you tell when squirrels are in love?

They go nuts for one another!

Q48.

What did the man with a broken leg tell his Valentine?

I have a crutch on you.

Q49.

What did the coffee say to the sugar on Valentines Day?

ANSWER

I love you a latte!

Q50.

What did two balls of yarn say when its Valentines day

ANSWER

Wool you be mine?

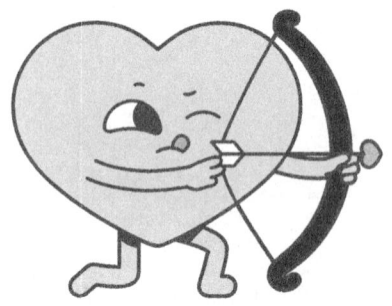

VALENTINES
day riddles

Get ready for some EPIC fun with riddles.

The next few pages feature fun Valentine's Day Riddles for kids From cheeky cupids to sweet surprises, these playful puzzles add joy to the festivities.

And off we go!

R1.

I am a tiny, flying creature known for shooting arrows. Who am I?

R2.

I am a sweet treat, covered in chocolate, and often given on Valentine's Day. What am I?

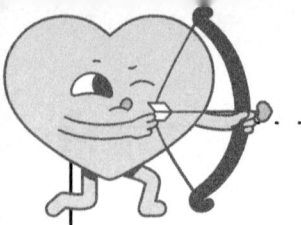

R3.

I am a fluffy, cuddly companion often given as a gift.

What am I?

R4.

I am a beautiful, fragrant bloom given to express affection. What am I?

R5.

I am a small, shiny piece of jewelry worn on the finger.
What am I?

R6.

I am a gesture of love, exchanged between two people.
What am I?

R7.

I am a little note expressing affection, exchanged on Valentine's Day. What am I?

R8.

I am a flying insect associated with love and often seen in gardens. What am I?

R9.

I am a red, heart-shaped fruit often associated with love. What am I?

R10.

I am a small, winged creature known for fluttering around flowers. What am I?

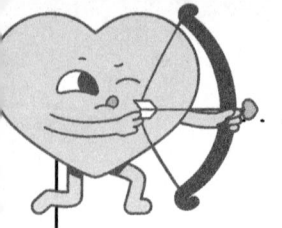

R11.

I am a gesture of commitment, often exchanged on Valentine's Day. What am I?

R12.

I am a small, cute creature that says "I love you" when I purr. What am I?

R13.

I am one of the primary colors of Valentines Day and I am the color of a rose. What am I?

R14.

I am a special day dedicated to expressing love and affection. What am I?

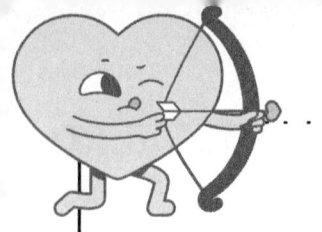

R15.

I am a red, heart-shaped symbol that represents love. What am I?

R16.

I am a delicious treat that comes in a heart-shaped box. What am I?

R17.

I am a type of jewelry worn around the neck, often given as a romantic gift. What am I?

R18.

I am a musical instrument known for playing love songs. What am I?

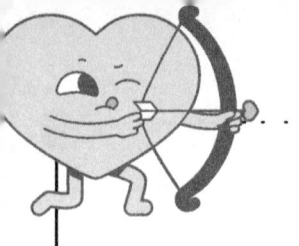

R19.

I am a small, mischievous creature associated with love and arrows. What am I?

R20.

I am a warm and fuzzy feeling that you get when you're in love. What am I?

R21.

I am a bunch of flowers that you give to your date. What am I?

R22.

I am a piece of paper with a special message written on it. What am I?

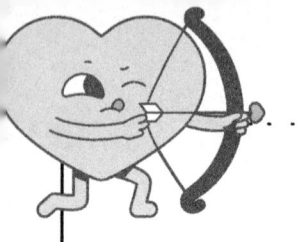

R23.

I am a beautiful gemstone often used in jewelry to symbolize love. What am I?

R24.

I am a colorful flowy decoration often seen on Valentine's Day, representing love. What am I?

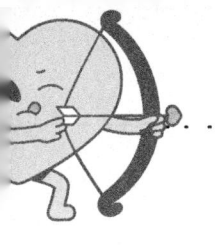

R25.

What travels around the world for Valentine's Day, but just stays in one corner?

R26.

I am a small, cuddly toy often given as a token of affection. What am I?

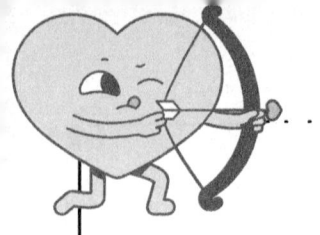

R27.

I am a form of communication that expresses love without words. What am I?

R28.

I am a sweet drink made from milk and flavored syrup, often enjoyed on Valentine's Day. What am I?

R29.

I am a shiny piece of jewelry worn on the wrist. What am I?

R30.

I can be touched, but can't be seen? What am I?

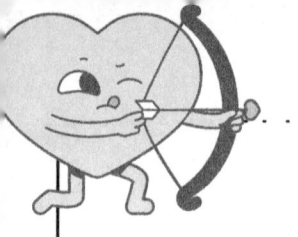

R31.

I am a small fluffy pastry and dessert that comes in various flavors and colors. What am I?

R32.

I am a small, winged insect known for making a buzzing sound. What am I?

R33.

I am a small, red fruit often used to make sweet jams and jellies. What am I?

R34.

I am a piece of art created to express love and admiration. What am I?

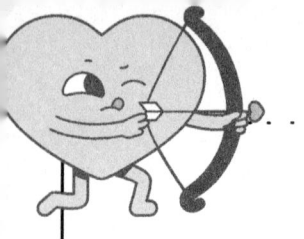

R35.

I am a cozy activity enjoyed on Valentine's Day, often involving blankets and Netflix or Hulu. What am I?

R36.

I am a game often played on Valentine's Day where you match pairs. What am I?

R37.

I am a warm and comforting beverage often enjoyed on a chilly day. What am I? Hot cocoa!

R38.

I am a delightful smell associated with love, often found in flowers. What am I?

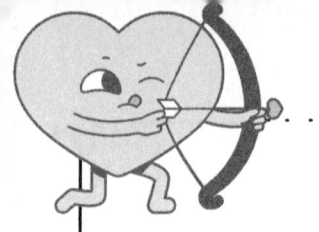

R39.

I am a playful expression of love, often exchanged through teasing or poking fun. What am I?

R40.

I am a chocolate round candy that has peanut butter in it and a lot of E's in the name? What am I?

R41.

I am a type of candy that's usually red and white with a sweet taste

R42.

I am a cute and cuddly creature often associated with affection. What am I?

R43.

I am a special moment shared between two people in love. What am I?

R44.

I am a shiny accessory often given as a romantic gift. What am I?

R45.

I am a delicious treat that is made with milk and frozen that can be eaten in a bowl or cone. What am I?

R46.

I am a small, portable music player that holds special love songs. What am I?

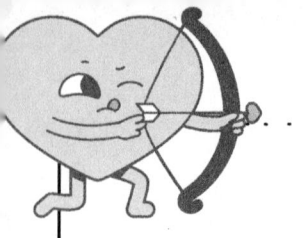

R47.

I am a decorative item often used to celebrate love and romance or birthday parties. What am I?

R48

Iam a symbol of love, often red and shaped like a heart. What am I?

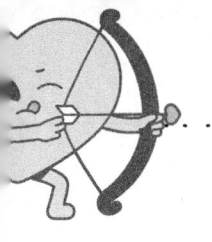

R49.

You'll find me in a bee, in a comb, in cakes, in a bunch, in a bun and even in mustard. What am I?

R50.

I am green and something you use to get Valentines Day Gifts.

RIDDLE ANSWERS

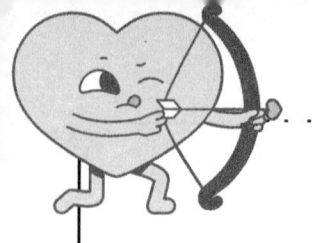

RIDDLE ANSWERS

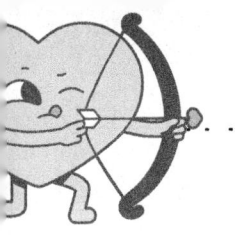

1. Cupid
2. A chocolate-covered strawberry
3. A teddy bear
4. A rose
5. A ring
6. A kiss
7. A love letter
8. A butterfly
9. A strawberry
10. A hummingbird
11. A promise ring
12. A kitten!
13. The color Red
14. Valentine's Day!
15. A balloon!

RIDDLE ANSWERS

16. Chocolates
17. A necklace
18. A violin
19. Cupid
20. Butterflies in your stomach
21. A bouquet
22. A love note
23. A ruby
24. Streamers
25. A stamp
26. A stuffed animal
27. Hugs
28. Strawberry milkshake
30. A heart

RIDDLE ANSWERS

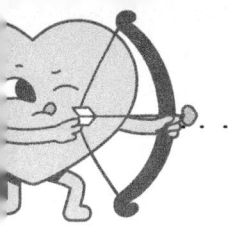

31. Cupcakes
32. A bee!
33. Cherries
34. A handmade card
35. A movie night
36. Memory game
37. Hot cocoa!
38. Fragrance!
39. A joke
40. Reese's peanut butter cup
41. A peppermint
42. A puppy
43. A hug
44. Earrings
45. Ice cream!

RIDDLE ANSWERS

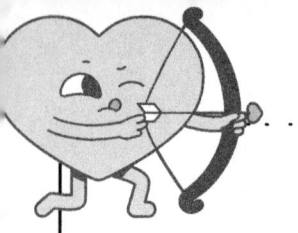

46. A playlist!
47. Heart-shaped balloons
48. A Valentine's Day card
49. Honey
50. Money

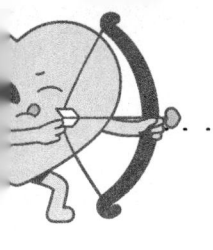

THANK YOU FOR YOUR PURCHASE

Heartfelt thanks for choosing my Valentine's Day Jokes and Riddles Book for Kids!

Your thoughtful purchase brings smiles and laughter to young hearts.

Your support means the world to me, and I hope the book adds joy to your Valentine's Day celebration. Grateful for your kindness and enthusiasm!

Printed in Great Britain
by Amazon